CW01640913

KHADIJAH IBRAHIIM

ROOTZ RUNNIN

inscribe

PEEPAL TREE

First published in Great Britain in 2008
by Inscribe an imprint of
Peepal Tree Press Ltd
17 King's Avenue
Leeds LS6 1QS
England

ISBN13: 9781845230593

Peepal Tree gratefully acknowledges Arts Council support

CONTENTS

Acknowledgements

I would like to acknowledge and give thanks to the creator for guiding me to write poems that root family and friends in the history of Leeds and the African Diaspora.

To my mother, grandmother and grandfather, aunties Dana and Dahlia for their shared stories. My brothers and sisters, my children, Jadey, Rheima and Ali, whose love keeps me going. Also to Jeremy Poynting and staff at Peepal Tree Press – Hannah Bannister, Dorothea Smartt and Kadija George for their encouragement and support. To Paulette Morris, Desiree Reynolds, Oluseyi Ogunjobi, and Lisa Blanchette for keeping me grounded with the truth. One love.

Dedicated to the loving memory of Mushea Hitchman

AFRO & 'FRO WEARING BROTHAS & SISTAHS (1970s)

Calling all
Afro and 'Fro wearing
brothas and sistahs

Calling all
Afro and 'Fro wearing
brothas and sistahs

Remember how the 1970s made us ride
on a conscious vibe?
Afros were picked way high
like Angela Davis's Black Power fist

Afros were antennas in the sky
connecting history's bloodline
tangled through triangle trade-lines

So old man river don't cry for me
We'll be forever loving Jah

Jah elevated a new NATION
now declaring they're stayin in Britain
where Afro and 'Fro wearing people

heard the call and said
Let freedom ring
By any means necessary

Calling all
Afro and 'Fro wearing,
brothas and sistahs

Calling all
funkadelic
soul conscious,
get down on it people

Calling all righteous
and understanding people...
What!
Hold-on... Wait a minute...
OVERS...
OVERstanding,
roots and culture
natty dread-wearing
brothas and sistahs.

Calling all
pimps and pimped out
street hookers,
and mothers and fathers
and mothers whose babies
got no fathers
because of the System,
the pressure the Eurocentric ideals
that's got brothas
crawling between prison walls,
pumped up on being the lesser,
down, down, down in life
asking, dear God

Where is the love?
Where is the love?

Calling brothas and sistas
who stand long
on Garvey's dream
sing Robert Nestor Marley

Kinky reggae
Kinky reggae now

Remember the Man Shaft

Shut yah mouth....you damn right

Wait!
Remember his smooth
ebony body,
his high sheen
Afro,
he was groomed
in *all* the right places
He just had some sistahs wanting
…just got this sistah thinking…

Calling all brothas and Idrins
who turned kung fu kicks
in cobbled back streets
allegiant to the Panthers
the Brotherhood, living the struggle

while politicians, held National Front positions,
teachers taught Columbus
preached straight hair Jesus
believing, WE did not know

WE,
in tune with
all Afro wearing
brothas and sistahs
who fought for our freedom and rights

That's why I'm calling
…and I'm calling and I'm still calling

and why the hell not?
Isn't this an
Afro wearing
time we live in

or what?

A SNAPSHOT HISTORY OF LEEDS

56 Cowper Street

As Grandma said,
New broom sweep clean
but the old one knows all the corners,
so brick by brick
I rebuild a house that once stood in Chapeltown,
56 Cowper Street,
a Victorian terrace with a green front door,
my grandparent's home,
where I slid down the staircase bannister
into laughter and now in memory.

I try to remember all things special,
like the Canadian gift of an oil painted portrait
of my dad and Aunt Sylvia
hanging against midnight-blue
circle-print wallpaper in the lounge;
Grandma's rose-porcelain tea sets;
her crystal and dust-free silverware,
for viewing only.

This seven-bedroom house signified
Importance in the ready hands of my
Jamaican family, blood spiced with Africa
and something of the colonial past.

Grandma grew roses and dahlias
in the front garden, picked gooseberries
to make jam and wine; Grandad dug tuff dirt
in the back yard, planted potatoes and cabbage.
Their tea they sipped from ceramic mugs,
blue for Grandad, red for Grandma,
except on special occasions, when Granny liked

a teacup with saucer.
Every day full-cooked breakfast from the kitchen –
nutmeg spiced condensed milk,
smoothed cornmeal porridge,
salt fish and callaloo, fried dumplings –
filled hungry bellies;
and the ritual of meals
at the oak dining-room table
with family and familiar friends
each with a story from which lessons
were to be learnt, now brings smiles.

Homespun

My stays at Cowper Street were long –
sometimes up to a year of Grandma's 'kidnap' –
to compensate for my father being overseas,
so I was split between
my mother's looser apron strings
and Grandma homespun rules
of do's and don'ts and decency,
when chores were regular and never shirked
for skipping ropes, jacks and hot rice,
when skylarking carried the repercussion of :
Stand up straight, pull your socks up!
Never mind de playing outside wid dem
pickney. Dem favour leggo beast.
Go find a book and read.
At Cowper Street,
love's strict hand nurtured studies,
mental arithmetic and recitation on the spot,
but Grandma also styled party frocks
on the Singer in her bedroom
and quilted the foundations of our kinship
for generations; told me of her Welsh-blooded grandfather,
Jabez, who gambled away the family's Jamaican land,

and of her first and second husbands,
her six children: five names beginning with the letter 'D',
the first born with an 'S';
these stories stitched tightly to me.

Home schooled

In my aunties' bedroom, the world moved
to the heartbeat of *I'm black and I'm proud*.
Aunty Dana and Dahlia wore natural hairstyles
cut pepper-grain short, combed smooth,
their stereo player played
soul melodies of Curtis Mayfield
We got to have peace,
and the reggae revolution of Steel Pulse
stirred their words.
Their bedroom walls carried through the atmosphere,
posters of Garvey, Ras Daniel Heartman's natty roots children,
and the Jackson Five, with their doctorates in Afros.

Combing through the thickness
of my little girl plaits, Aunty Dahlia tied satin ribbons,
left them long to dangle to my neck.
Aunty Dana spoke of ancestry,
African empires before Hawkins sailed in greed,
gave me the gift of their narratives
and books for my birthdays –
on Harriet Tubman and her soldier stance –
books not seen in schools.
They educated me.

Grandad's Home brew

In the front room, whether indigo skies
or a rainy grey covered the afternoons,

Grandad hammered bottle caps onto homemade brew,
welding metal caps onto brown glass bottles
as he listened to Beethoven's symphonies,
or sang folk songs with mento rhythms
like *River bank Coverly, River to the bank Coverly...*
paced to match the speed of his work.

The taste of beer already bottled
would wet the mouths of Will Ruddock,
Valentine and Winifred Daley
who synchronised visits to slam dominoes
to wood, and fire up games of Ludo.
And more big people brought talk,
not always for a child to hear,
their tongues navigating the West Indies,
stretching back to Paul Bogle's Jamaican revolt.

And within this room in Cowper Street
Grandad rallied the Brotherhood
like a rebel god, hungry to put
wrongs to right, reshape man's thinking,

4, Gathorne Mount

At 4 Gathorne Mount, our house,
mine when Grandma released the reins,
cooking pots crowned the stove-top daily,
smells of Mum peeling back skin from onions,
grating fresh ginger, mixing spices to season up meat,
life moved with a looser reggae beat.

It was five a we giggling pickney
who loved to ramp and play
Andrew, Leroy, Angela, me –
and late-born Damian. We never knew when time came
fe settle like a pot of kidney bean

in wait for bay leaf, thyme and coconut cream.
Mum always said:
Unoo favour heng pon nail,
and
Who caan't hear must feel
– plenty switch and belt beatings.

Though sometimes we had blues in the cellar,
where people came to rub-a-dub
under the Babycham-box 'lampshade',
there was no choice for Angela and me
when Sundays came. We had to
go to church with Mother Brown's
twins, Jackie and Janet and Miss Tiny's
grandaughter, Dionne, in our Sunday best,
memorise Hail Mary, pray for forgiveness,
go to confession, light candles for God's joy –
ours came from the incense of chicken,
rice and peas at home.
But Sunday's were also for dusting off
the smoked glass coffee table,
Lynch's Spanish Tina reproduction
and the lava lamp in the front room,
then getting a musical education from Mum
as we listened to U Roy's and Big Youth's dub versions
on the Blue Spot radiogram;
later, Al Green on *Soul Train* and Dorothy Moore's
Misty Blue on the new stereo.
That's when we pickney learnt to dance.

As often as we could, we escaped outside
through cobbled backstreets
that led down to the beck, for games
of British bull dog and hot rice.
We kids scraped knees, bled cuts to tears,
as regular as the news of the day

heard over gardens walls and washing lines
of who was doing what in marital affairs.

Back home, scuffed shoes and black pumps
kicked off, after a supper of Milo and toast,
we'd huddle beside the kitchen gas fire
to view a picture palette of only three stations
on our rental Rumbelow TV.
We liked how Black kept on the attack
in *Love Thy Neighbour*,
but *Black and White Minstrels*,
and Jim Davidson's 'Chalky',
with thick lips and big nose jokes,
were never found funny in our home.

Harehills Middle School

Young hearts shake hands cross cultures
feet masquerade in time to heart beats,
Lisa, Yasmin and show-off kids like me
danced the bump, played jacks and skipped
in the playground of Harehills Middle school.

But the real boastful kids were those in
Mrs Senior's dance class,
stars of Grey trophy high jump, long jump,
the netball and football team
Their triumphs at tournaments mapped ideas
of what we could be

In lessons at old wood desks
with redundant stained inkwells
(used by Uncle Douglas fifteen years before
when it was still a boys' school),
we read history books about William the Conqueror,
1066, the Tudors and Victorians;

fractions and algebra, never grasped fully,
though Math classes were slipper strict
in the hands of Mr Adkin.
High-tempered Mr Richmond
of the hairy face taught English,
threw words and pupils round the room.
Miss Taylor taught our hands
to curve to mould clay pots
– another ashtray to take home.

Sometimes we earned merits for excellence,
more often, detention or the cane.

Excitement rippled one morning assembly
when Mr Bramwell was due to announce
who'd won the brand new chopper bike
with a bell and tassels,
but first we had to say the Lord's prayer
and sing *Kumbayah, My Lord, Kumbayah*,
before Colleen Green and her brother Silas
were announced the winners.

Jammed with working class families
with very little, we kids
stirred crazy to collect old newspapers,
did sponsored runs and walked to a frenzy
to add to the school funds, win
all to gain house points
and win the trophy
for Red or Blue, Yellow or Green.

We were happy for halfpenny sweets
in a paper bag, Dainty toffees,
savoury vinegar crisps, Spanish and sherbet fountains
from the school tuck shop;
happy for youth clubs, seven inch vinyl

played on the Bush player with a tin pan sound;
we danced to Abba, Bay City Rollers and Michael Jackson,
wore Afros, flares, crocheted hats and plaits.

Sunday's top twenty on the radio brought anxious
youth to guess who's at number one
– before Thursday's Top of the Pops, *Smash Hits*
and *Jackie* magazine.
Remember when Third World's
Now that we found love
What are we gonna do with it?
got to number one?

And when ITV came to make
a documentary at the school,
they used the Third World hit
as the theme tune for the show –
Orlando Weeks at home and at school,
a family affair. And when we saw *Paradise Lost's*
film of Harehill's crumpled streets
on our TVs, we saw nothing *then* to regret;
for us kids nothing mattered but
the friends we made and the games we played.

Roots on TV

Oats porridge, hard-dough bread,
a snip of herb tea for breakfast:
I'd remember to wipe my mouth
at the bus stop on Roundhay Road
where I walked short Grace Jones Afro style,
black girl pride channelling my steps.
I rode two buses to Bramley Town End
just to get to school at Intake High.
During class registration
the teacher asked,

Who watched Roots on TV?
and me, the only black child in class,
screwed up my face,
kissed ma teeth at the classroom
laughter, cut my eye at
Janet Whitehouse sat next to me
scribbling National Front Party
on her desk; white girl pride.

At Intake School not one
hard-dough bread-eating kid in my class
just chips and beans
NF and British Movement followers
propelled spits, taunts in Yorkshire slang
slurred names: *Chocolate Drop,*
Nig Nog, Sambo, Jungle Bunny,
Golly Wog, Kizzy go home.

Union Jack

Mum always said she should have gone back home
when *Rivers of Blood* ran deep
in the current of Enoch Powell's hate
...the Tiber foaming with blood...
an urgent encouragement of re-emigration...

Send them back; load the ship with
chocolate smiles, send them back
before blacks take the whip hand...

No Blacks, No dogs, No Irish!
One down, a million to go!

But unoo barn hyah, Mum said.
I sweep the Union Jack
under the bed.

Youth Rage

We never imagined
the night rage burnt cars and shops,
rioting a stone's throw from my house.

Big youth, man and woman,
raged up a passion,
set out the streets like an arena
for a bull fight with the Babylon.
Fire! Fire! Disturbed hearts smashed
bricks through the smoky heat,
exploded against discrimination,
suss laws and racist attacks,
and inner city streets burnt to ash,
because there was 'f' all else to do
but sign on, get your UB40,
passport to collect the dole.

In our back-to-back and terraced houses
working-class black and white
youth played Snap!
Sex Pistols latched onto this white heat,
graffitied Elizabeth's head
stuck up two fingers, wore safety-pins
and spat on the Union Jack.
We watched them pogo dancing up and down
to The Clash's *white riot* of reggae-snatched rhythms,
while Maggie snatched milk
brought recession and the poll tax.
And when The Specials rocked against racism,
they marched right past my street
up to Potternewton Park
'til *its like a zebra crossing, black and white,*
black and white as far as you can see.

Black is black 1980s

UK
Black
is black
in we music –
the sounds yuh caan't claim –
mixing d' soul and gospel of Black America
and dee bass-line and drum talking outta Jamaica.
You caan't hold we down
we player of music,
we dancer, we singer.

It's just how we do it,
from front room parties
to basement's blues dance
all-dayers and all-nighters
rare reggae grooves,
James Brown's funk rhythms
that came right back
in d' break-beat,
d' loops da mixing down
house and hip hop
best foot moves –
tearing up d' warehouse parties.

We learnt d' funky chicken,
did the Wop, corked the *Wag Club*,
rocked in Doc Martens' boots,
Levi 501s, and balanced
flat caps over curly perms and extension plaits.

We moved against Thatcher's time,
flipped the script to come again
in UK street riots.

We talked the blues
Talking blues, keep on talking blues
They say your feet is just too big for your shoes...

From the underground,
DJ's called up the elements:
sound-system dance,
Kiss FM,
Funky Dread's
Soul 2 Soul
with tumping bass,
while Black and British
voice of an angel, Caron Wheeler
smoothed the heat,
kept us moving
back to life,
back to reality.

We African
we African Caribbean
we Black
we Black and British,
however we want it to be
we ride pon de riddim
wheel back de version
sound system styleee... and, into the 90s...

There's nothing like this...
Sip a glass of cold champagne wine...
there's nothing like this...

THE CROWNING

Empress, dread queens, kings,
children of the African diaspora
come draw your circle of listeners.

Speak your truth on legacy of empire, church,
enslaved packed ships where ancestors
were tossed like pebbles into the ocean.

Come warriors, soul rebels,
singers of the blues, spirits of the purple dawn,
bring us Solomon's bigger history,

for we are readers, pen-stressors
dust blowers from basement libraries,
knowledge stackers and frequent travellers.

In the natural mystic breeze, we are dee lion,
in the whirlwind we are dee flag –
the red black green of it.

In Garvey's starliner
we connect the mediums
beyond the ships.

Bring your melodies, songs makers,
chants and dance; reclaim we name
and bury the pain.

Bring to the ceremonies clay pots,
calabashes, incense and oils,
tell de people dem fe come,

come with their head wraps
and ginny heads, come with their cornrows,
Afros and their natty dread.

Bring harmony and comeliness and
the Wisdom in your navel string,
Bring the ancient prescriptions:

bring priests, drums, silk white robes,
burn seven oils in seven corners for seven days,
read nine psalms of David without ceasing.

Come purify we so we recognise
the Conquering Lion
of the tribe of Judah

Jah Ras Tafari
Jah Ras Tafari
Jah Ras Tafari

DANCEHALL POEMS

(In the 1990s the roots & culture, back to Afrika movement seemingly faded in the voices of the dancehall DJ's. Raggamuffin gold teeth, slackness talk and ghetto fabulous became the anthem, and lyrical gun Don and Mr Lover Man clashed for the title of Don Gorgon, & Donnette for the title of Dancchall Queen.)

Dancehall Sound Clash

I reminisce on heartical times
when Sir Coxson did rub-a-dub
with cool vibes, an' Saxon
toast bonafide bionic rhymes.

I reminisce dancehall 1980's style
with an exodus of speaker boxes
in old vans ready to line walls
at Chapeltown Community Centre,

where wires spiral through soundman hands,
connect dread man at de control
with turntable, amplifier and tweeter
an selected sounds of Mama Africa's sons:

Marley, Tosh, D Brown, Jacob Miller,
Jamrock raw roots reggae riddims:
Do you know what it means to have a revolution?
Fighting against downpression.

In the height of sound clash
Manchester and Leeds strike a match
Baron high power came to test tunes
Sparta sound boy head dem swell.

In London King Tubby came too,
dropped dub plates inna de dance.
But Jungle Warrior crew got fresh
with a deeper cylinder-charge in the bass-line.

Revolutionary sounds of rasta
weaved through head wraps,
beaver hats, red, gold and green tams,
and dreams of the promised land.

Irie skanking lean foot youths
in Clarks' heels and Bally brand boots,
Sistrens in pencil pleated skirts,
armed with passion eena rub a dub dance,

lick wood, praise Jah, summons
order to selecta fe *Lift it up,*
pull it back, come again.
In dis I and I reminisce.

Ram Dance Master

Dancehall
deejay
ram dance
master
wid yah crew-cut fade,
etched dollar sign, razor sharp
S-curls and waves under de du-rag,
a true,
a you
de people dem prefer.

Set for
water pumpy,
cool and deadly
freedom floods dance floors
so hot, so pepper
in de heat of the night
sleng teng dancing
till a dawn,

de Selecta spins vinyl
fresh studio cut crackling smooth
riddim ease through bass line,
gathering sing jays, deejays
lyrical Dons
toasting in season,
over de tune.

Nuff man and woman
jus-a heng on
dem jus-a sway
and na ride de riddim.

Gyal hold tight to boasty mouth
of Shabba Ranks' *world of girls*,
Tingalingaling, school bell ring,
dis yah lover man is praised
in de current of hand waves.

Words clash at de microphone stand as
Tiger Man, Cutty Ranks,
Ninja Man recite odes,
an de twenty-one gun-talk
of de Dons cuffing Sound boys
triggers sound salute.
Dons big bout yah in de sea of de night ravers
bawl forward to reeewind

Haul and pull it, Selecta
and come back again.

Dancehall Deejay,
ram dance master
wid u crew-cut and fade
dollar marking pencilled
razor sharp and slick and click suit,
a true, a you, a you, a you, a you
de people dem prefer.

Dancehall Queen

Donnette, dancehall queen
Butterfly's knock-kneeing style
and pattern, her fashion de latest
outa New York, Paris and London, the originator
of Jamdown ghetto fabulous,
royalty hot-footing dancehall
arenas, flexing blue, pink, green,
and yellow peacock hair weaves,
gold teeth, diamond crepe,
Miss Wire Waist, mampi batty riding
glamour at its best, Dj's crown her
Dancehall Queen,
Donnette reigns supreme.
She naar jest.

BIRD OF AFRICA

Here I come again,
like a bennu riding on the wind,
crossing oceans to dock on river banks
between the mangroves.
Here I come, five hundred years of
pinioned wings stretching
into the Gambian sea
of *barakas, djembi* drum calls,
into the hot wet air I fly.

Here I sweat away
a stolen past, slake a throat
parched from dusty red roads
alighting to hot tin roofs, thatched mud huts
and sweltering nights,
servings of bread (and the strange look
of bush meat), retreating from the rain of white flies
while the river embraces the sunset melodies
of Garnet Silk, *Hello mama Africa how are you?*
Play, pause, press rewind three times
Watch the moonlit water flicker,
scratch away the pain of mosquitos
welcoming me home.

It feels like yesterday,
pulling back the curtain of the past
to hear the griot singing for the healing
of five hundred broken years
20 million or more stolen voices
from the motherland.

DAYS UNFOLD A NEW BEGINNING

…birds wishing to share the fruits of love …

Days unfold a new beginning
in a season of migration,
two birds fan wings in unison
make sweet liquid sounds in the sky,
seductively steal each other's hearts.
Radiant as a peacock's tail,
longing to fly, she flaps passionately
to see if greener grass grows across the pond.
He nestles in the windy city
between soft poetic notes,
smoky skyscrapers,
highways, trains and bridges.

Two birds of fantasy twitter
day and night to rearrange
the direction of the crescent moon
in favour of exotic desires.
Love's stream narrows
into a whirlpool; rain brews;
a senseless cold breeze blows,
arouses a hot and fiery ring,
melts wings in peppery winds;
fists of thunder knock
as heaven's hands clap.
In a crazy flight of fancy
two birds wheel and turn.
Now they flutter through photo galleries
asking with whom lies the fault,
only to seek a different beginning
a new beginning, the bittersweet
taste of love.

KINDRED

Curly Locks,
your mudda is a dreadlocks,
woman with fire and wind
burning red, gold and green,
cowrie shells in her hand.
Her spirit comes from maroon blood
and Oya must have given her the wind
when she talk and walk.

With Jah love in her heart
she bring you come
inna de night when all asleep.

True you favour your mudda eena da eyes,
but you have your daddy's kinks and locks
and his round cherry smile, God Merciful and Kind,
Raheem, princess soon to be queen.

And down de line Great Granny comes with coconut oil
and Nanna with green Dax to wax your plaits
with stories of Great Granny Ujena,
who stood no taller than five feet,
and I with oils, sandalwood and butter of cocoa
come to anoint your crown
so your dreads drink oils made
since Eve and our beginnings.

WE BURY OUR DEAD

My mother's hands
bound family ties
near and far,
pick up
a long distance call
to bury our dead.

Jamaica cries
Kingston's sadness sweats tears:
six gun shots to the head
a grandson dead.

Dusted hats and polished shoes in procession.
at Dovecot cemetery;
I gaze at satin, grey-beaded mules
stained to burnt orange,
dust licking crevices under the soles of feet.
Preacher man says:
We must love our brother.
The Lord God is our saviour.
And the choir sings over the coffin.
Loved ones swell tears into red dirt.
We bury our dead.

Watery smiles from kinfolk
and friends with tales of what used to be
and better must come.
Rum offerings pour from hands to honour the departed,
bring duppy stories, and dancing tongues
lash white rum. We bury our dead.

Gun shots burn red Kingston's heat,
at Dovecot cemetery. A polished procession:
preacher man, choir, loved ones and bronze shining coffin.

Into red dirt we tears swell,
wet eyes guide heaven's gates.
We pray, we bury our dead.

At the corner of life
my mother's arms bring us together.
I hear Jamaica cry, long distance call,
to bury our dead.

WHEN MY TIME COME

'The lord is my shepherd I shall not want,
He lays me down to sleep in green pastures'

Mi dear chile,
we are livin' in our last days
so when mi time come,
I waant to be buried in mi red suit,
the one I just buy.

I buy a new one every five years
just for de occasion,
I like to keep with the fashion
and dis suit favour de roses in my garden –
you know how I love dem so.

So look here, child,
when mi time come I waant you
to remember
dis is de suit I waant to be buried in,
de red one right here,
trailing from neck to hem
wid beads and silk embroidery
just like royalty,
a colour of importance.
I saw de queen wearing one just like it pon TV.

So remember wat mi show you;
see how it tailor stitched in and out
with good threads,
like mi granny use to do.
She bury in red too.

And when de Lord calls
I want to be wearing a red suit,

de one I handpick especially –
I walk de whole day till carn bun mi toes.

I like to look good at all times,
no-one is going to say
I never dress away till de end of my days.
Mi buy mi suit from Marks and Spencer,
all mi underwear too,
put dem in de trunk
with all mi fine nightwear and tings,
fold in camphor balls.
Mi a ole woman 75 years just gone,
but mi a no fool,
mi make all mi plans;
put down insurance
fe horse-drawn carriage,
gospel singers, saxophone player,
and a red rose for each and every one.

Mi no waant bury a England
mi waant mi ashes spread cross de River
Thames, make de waves teck
mi back to which part mi did come from.

And when all and sundries come to the house,
start dig, stake claim to what dem waant,
to wat dem no waant,
when tears flare and tongues clash difference,
I want my daughter to remember
dis is the red suit I waant to be buried in,

the red one right here.